A H

FOR

# FINDING YOUR WAY

AFTER

Loss and Grief
Divorce and Relationship Breakups
Injury and Illness
Financial Distress

*By GINA CANNONE*
Master Clinical Hypnotherapist
Reiki Master Teacher
Life & Spiritual Coach
Spiritualist
Ordained Minister

IbbiLane Press
Copyright

ISBN-9780578621395

# DEDICATION

*This book is dedicated to all those that I have
crossed paths with, that came to
me for healing and for guidance.*

*Through healing others, I have become
a better person and
truly passionate about the work I do.*

*I thank all of you for trusting in me!*

*ALSO, to my sister Denise who
inspired me to share my learnings and abilities to rebuild life
after many of my own life's difficulties.*

The purpose of this book is to help and guide those who may be
facing difficult life changes.
Needing solutions, answers, and ways to cope.

To understand that you can hurdle and push through, rebuild and
start a new life, as I have had
to do.

This book is for those who need a handbook of help to ease one
through difficult transitions of life…

# TABLE OF CONTENTS

# FOREWORD(s)

I've always admired and tried to learn from individuals that are happy; people that have good energy and a positive spirit; how do they overcome difficult challenges and what do they do differently that helps them live a joyful, fulfilling, and happy life?

The moment I met GIna I knew she was one of those people, that despite some very difficult life experiences she has adapted and learned to change herself. How wonderful is it to be surrounded by joyful friends, who are positive and just know that despite their own challenges, are praying for YOU and for your own happiness. Gina truly understands the joy of working hard, self-discovery, and helping others. She always has a plan, continues each and every day to adapt, grow and build her skills. Her book Finding Your Way is Gina's personal journey.

If you're feeling stuck or just want to continue on your own journey of becoming a better person to live a joyful life, this book is easy to understand and implement. The book helps break down overwhelming or complex situations into simple steps of how to take your own personal life lessons, learn from them, and turn them into a positive situation. There are times in my life that I have felt lost or hopeless and like Gina, know there is something positive to learn in every worst situation. No one wants to feel stuck but if you do, this book provides simple tools to become unstuck; and how to change, grow, and live again. A life of positivity, prayer, faith in God and living life to our fullest potential is the greatest gift we can give ourselves and those around us.

Be happy and keep smiling, for those around us will also feel our joy.

Linda Lutkevich


I haven't known Gina for very long, but out connection was immediate.  She is an authentic person who lives the words she writes. She emanates strength and clarity and takes action to get what she needs and move away from anything that hinders her.  Her advice in this book is spot on and delivered from a place of first-hand experience.  She understands deeply the topics she covers in this book.

As I stated in my first sentence, I haven't known Gina for very long, but have worked side by side with her for over a year now.  She is the real deal, never wavering, deeply spiritual and generous with her gifts. Prepare to receive exactly what you need in the pages of this book.

Norma Tolliver

# AUTHOR'S PREFACE

Most of us will face many of life's difficulties, life's painful experiences, re-examining our lives, dealing with circumstances that we are not prepared for and then must learn how-to cope and get through them. Life can be going along beautifully, joyfully, and then like a bullet to the chest-tragedy strikes; Illness, Death of a loved one, Relationship breakups/divorce, loss of job or business.

Life changes can be both positive and negative. Throughout your life, you will deal with many of life's changes. Some will be easier than others to get through.  This book is about *the choices we have and can make* to help get through these difficult circumstances.  This book is also about *maintaining a strong faith in GODS plan for us*.

Stress levels during these changes are extremely elevated and can cause other health issues.  Learning how to manage your stress will help stabilize your physical, mental and emotional health. People who resist change and resist coping with the issues, may experience greater stress, along with other negative physical and psychological effects.

I have had to face and get through many difficult and extreme life changes.  I felt compelled to write how I not only made it through, but how I *became complete and whole again*. Free from the fear, worry, stress.

I lost my husband tragically at age 46, he was 56.  I moved three times, re-adjusting to life without him.  My mother-my best friend passed a few years later.  Grief on top of grief, was painful, immobilizing, and seemed like there was no doorway to peace from this.  Constant, stress was residing inside me.  One year later, I was rushed to Sloan, for a tumor on my ovary. They told me I had ovarian cancer. I went through the surgery and a miracle happened, it was not cancer and I truly got blessed. I experienced a "White Light" and a "Vision" prior to surgery and peacefulness came over me. I did not know I would witness a miracle, but I did. Experiencing this changed my life. I was grateful, humbled and now I never take a moment for granted. TIME means everything to me. LIFE means everything to me. FAITH means everything to me.

Your mind can make you crazy when your life is re-routed. I sought out help, therapy, bereavement, and then Reiki and Hypnotherapy. Hypnosis worked tremendously for healing. Removing negative thought patterns to replacing them with positive ones. Letting go of painful images through neuro-linguistic programming (NLP) and eye movement therapy (EMT) helped tremendously in my healing process. This freed me from so much, that I decided to become a Master Hypnotherapist, so I could help others too.

My family and friends have always admired my strength and coping abilities to move forward. To me it felt like survival of the fittest. I was either going to sink deep into despair, depression, and fear or swim to the surface, breath new air, regain my health, strength, and find a new path, more purposeful and rebuild a new life, my new life…

This book is meant to help you cope, heal, find strength, as I have, and to help you find your way back into life!
To feel like yourself again and free to live again…

Love & Light

*Gina Cannone*

# INTRODUCTION

So, what is hopelessness? Beyond optimism or hope, desperate, despairing: hopeless grief, without hope, impossible to accomplish, solve, resolve. Not able to learn or act, perform, or work as desired. Despondent. Hopeless feelings, dread and anxiety.

Why can some escape the black hole, and others drift deeper into despair? I believe that individuals that can reframe and restructure their thoughts, understand and think about what *it will require*, to come out of the despair; will and become determined too. Remaining hopeless is unhealthy, drains good energy, and increases depression, stress and anxiety. I did not like being in that state of grief, hopelessness, fear of future, and abandonment. I desperately wanted my mind back, a life back, and had to first make that decision before any further steps were to be taken.

Through difficult life changes, life seems; distorted, meaningless, fearful. The questions start to haunt you: What am I going to do now? How can I change this? Why did this happen? What ifs? The day must come to take your mind back. STOP the what ifs! Accepting the circumstance and releasing that question is a must for healing. It may take time-but that thought needs to be put to rest. One positive step leads to the next, and it is one step at a time.

Seeking therapy for healing is essential and highly beneficial to your overall well-being. If suicidal thoughts are present, seek medical care immediately. Nothing is worth taking your own life, and it is very easy to think life is not worth living when suffering from extreme trauma, changes and loss. Protect your health and take your time to think things through. There is light at the end of all, even if you feel there isn't. I *never lost faith* through my suffering. Always praying for answers, guidance, and relief of any kind.

I can honestly say, what I have endured has made me a better person. I have become a "new" me and I am proud of my survival and coping skills, I never knew I had. The chapters to follow will help you overcome and survive your storms of life. The mind is quite powerful. It can keep you down or move you forward onto new paths. You can choose the direction.

All sorts of feelings arise through life's challenges. Deep despair, usually comes when diagnosed with a serious, life-threatening illness and during the aging process, focusing on age and death. When health seems to be on the decline you can feel powerless and hopeless. When my doctors diagnosed me with ovarian cancer, stage 3, I felt immediate despair and suicidal thoughts. I was instantly put into a panic anxiety ridden state of mind. When learning after surgery that I did not have any cancer, was a true blessing and what we all believed was a miracle. What if I did commit suicide based on the facts prior to surgery? I admit, I thought about it…Why have the surgery? I should just kill myself. My family and friends held my hand, calmed me down and said I must have the surgery no matter what the outcome later.

Feelings of entrapment in a relationship you feel you can't leave; feelings of not having self-worth, or confidence to leave and begin life alone. I have done this a few times, left relationships that I knew I had to. Even if great love was present, leaving was the best and most difficult choice. The empowerment you feel when you make the choice and not leave it to someone else, or wait for the change that never happens, is beyond great. Once you make the decision, then act upon it, you instantly feel a sense of relief, power, motivation, control of your life and direction. Grief is different kind of devastation. Losing a loved one is heart wrenching. Losing someone to a tragic and sudden death is shocking and traumatic. Shock symptoms set in; disbelief about the death, it can feel like a bad dream, and the physical symptoms can include; shaking, crying, screaming, immobilization-creating an inability to speak, eat, drink or sleep. Aches and pains, anxiety, headaches, stomach aches, heart palpitations (as if having a heart attack) can come and go.

When I found out about my husbands' tragic death, I immediately was in shock. I thought someone was playing a joke on me, but realized it wasn't. I was alone and managed to call my mother, but no words would come out of my mouth. She heard me crying, but no words. I heard her saying what's wrong, what's wrong. Still no words. She lived around the corner on the next block, and I heard her say we'll be right there. Even when my parents showed up - I could not speak. I understand fully now the steps it takes to overcome sudden loss, and the healing process that is needed to get back in the world again, to live and enjoy life again.

In this book, I will go into depth on how I overcame many difficult life changes, and the steps I took for protecting my own personal health, for rearranging my life, beginning new paths, and creating a "new" me. Removing guilt, fear, stress, anxiety, depression and grief.

I live what I teach. I live fearlessly, with deep spiritual faith and belief that I am guided and protected.

Accepting life's curves of cruelty, life's precious time, and appreciating the joy and beauty of life fully.

If you are having trouble overcoming and going forward from any life changing circumstances, then the following chapters will help you learn how to gain control back, work towards a new future and begin a new journey.

*"When we are no longer able to change a situation, We are challenged to change ourselves."*

Viktor E Frankl

# CHAPTER 1

## FACING CHANGES

No one said it was going to be easy to accept and overcome the challenges and disruptions within the course of life. But no one prepared us either. Life is wonderful when things are going our way, moving ahead, dreams are coming true, business is great, and all seems to be perfect. Even if you think you are ahead of the game, knowing the next move, life can come at you like a tsunami; unexpected, a turn for the worse, a disruption, a traumatic event that stops you in time. Facing and trying to understand the external event of change; loss of a loved one, loss of a pet/a job/career, end of relationship or marriage, business failure, serious illness or any other traumatic event, can send you into a deep depression and paralyze you with fear.

Facing new life changes requires us to let go; of the past, the person we lost, the familiar place we were used to, the life we once had, the way things were, and start new. How can we, when we are stricken with panic, fear, and anxiety about entering the unknown? How will we possibly move forward?

FACING and OVERCOMING GRIEF…

This is what seemed so hard for me. I had life all figured out, things were great, and that one phone call where I was told that my husband had a fatal accident, changed it all in a second. Time seems to stop, your heart feels ripped out of you, and shock sets in. Sudden loss is a shock to your system which can create a rippling effect of symptoms and ailments such as; headaches, shaking, uncontrollable crying, stomach aches, sleeping issues, increased feelings of isolation, depression, anxiety, abandonment, along with guilt and anger. Grief is a natural response to pain and loss, and we must endure it. Take all the time you need to grieve. Do not let anyone tell you otherwise. Everyone grieves in their own way, at their own pace. We may be left with unanswered questions, why? how? and wishing we did something more, better, different, but soon you will realize that you must leave those thoughts behind or they will cripple you.

If you are not functioning in day to day living after a length of time that *you* feel is too long, then you must seek medical/professional help. The process takes time and it's different for everyone. We know in due time that we will overcome the pain and loss. There is an end to mourning. Having a strong faith and belief helps with the healing process. Be patient, for healing happens gradually.

Facing the challenges and the changes after mourning eventually becomes a reality. Months may have gone by, even years. Many questions begin to swirl your mind…What should I do? Should I sell the house? Where do I move to? How will I live without them? What am I supposed to do?

What helped me through this was listening to people whose opinions I respected. My mother, and dear friends held my hand, watched over me, and guided me. You tend to not think clearly, and it's extremely difficult to make decisions. These are life changing decisions and fear of the unknown is also swirling in your mind that makes this more difficult.

HELPFUL ADVICE for GRIEF RECOVERY:

- There is no right or wrong way to grieve, take your time.
- Seek help from the people who care for you.
- Seek medical/professional help if suicidal thoughts or severe depression occurs.
- Grief will trigger many unexpected emotions. Embrace them, allow them to happen.
- Join a bereavement or support group.
- Take better care of yourself through your grief, monitor your health, get check-ups.
- Acknowledge your pain, remind yourself it will get easier.
- Try not to isolate yourself-being around family and friends for support is essential for healing.
- Talk about your grief, even if in small doses.
- Prayer and Faith-can offer solace. Meditating, going to church, speaking to Clergy may help comfort you.
- Even though very difficult, try to maintain any hobbies or interests, so you can relax your mind for a while.
- Always do what is best for you…during holidays, birthdays, anniversary, visit for the time that is comfortable for you. Leave when you want, stay as long or a short as you feel like.
- It's ok and normal to laugh and enjoy moments during grief. Moving forward doesn't mean you will forget that person, the life you had. It's a way of acceptance and learning how to get your life back to a more normal, healthy state.

I have experienced both a sudden death, and my mother's death from cancer. I learned that the grief process was different for each passing. I went through all the stages of grief for the sudden loss of my husband, but not for my mother. I had closure with her. I got to hold her hand as she passed away and it was terrible and beautiful at the same time. A sudden, accidental, unexpected traumatic death occurs without warning or preparation. The grief process can be different and more intense, with many compounding issues.

During my grief stages, I realized I needed to come to terms with the losses. If not, I would drown. I was catching myself from entering deep depression. I had no will to eat, work, shower, or even live. Each day I decided to take a small step to entering the world again. Just going to the food store for fifteen minutes was what I remembered doing first. It was brutal, since my husband always did the food shopping. I didn't know where anything was and broke down crying in the store. Doing all the jobs he usually did was heart wrenching, exhausting and unbearable. Help from others only lasts a short time. They have their own life to tend to and you are eventually on your own. Secondary losses may include; loss of home, loss of income, loss of friends, loss of routine.

I ended up moving three times over the next 5 years. I found myself still in somewhat of disbelief that my life was so drastically changed. My mind and body directed me to heal. I could not cry or grieve anymore. I needed to feel better, to laugh, enjoy my friends, family, and just start my new life, whatever it was to be.

I realized I had complicated mourning and post-traumatic stress disorder from how my husband passed. He fell fifteen stories to his death, working on a balcony. The image was brutal, and I just could not get past it. I needed counseling and professional help. I joined a bereavement group and I had hypnosis and eye movement therapy

(EMDR) for removing the emotions attached to the images. I was then able to talk about the passing without crying or any emotions. It was such a relief and a blessing. My body had said - enough. Hypnotherapy helped me tremendously with my issues. I felt so good and relieved from my therapy sessions that I decided to go back to school and become a hypnotherapist myself, wanting to help others as well.

FACING and OVERCOMING SERIOUS ILLNESS...

Through my intense grief, I was forewarned that I was at a higher risk for illness from stress, anxiety, and trauma. Well, soon after my husband passed, my mother passed, then six months after that my biological father passed and the grief was compounded. A year went by and I just did not feel well. Tired, lethargic, unmotivated, lost again, depleting savings accounts for I had no energy to work, and trying hard to recover to become my old self. My stomach started extending over a four-day period and I knew I was sick. In disbelief about my health now, facing a serious issue, surgery, loss of more work, my stress, anxiety and fear was overwhelming. I walked myself into the hospital that day and was sent to Sloan in Manhattan. I was told I had stage 3 ovarian cancer and they immediately scheduled surgery that week. I prayed for everyone and myself, that was going through a life-threatening health issue. This was more than unbearable for me. I fell immediately into depression, suicidal thoughts were occurring, and I had intense feelings of hopelessness. My spiritual connection and belief remained strong. I prayed to (GOD), my husband, my mother, for any help at all. Praying for anything that would ease this situation and my mind.

I went into surgery, and upon awakening the Doctor stated I had won the lottery. He searched everywhere for cancer, there was none.  He said he had left me open to go to pathology himself, to see if there was a mistake made.  I felt I had a miracle occur.  I felt blessed and now compelled to help others.  I did have a tumor removed and a full radical hysterectomy.

During recovery, I realized even more how alone I was. I had help from friends and family, but I realized many things during that period. I truly had a spiritual awakening. I realized I needed to prepare and rearrange my life for comfort, peace and calmness. To remove ANYTHING that caused me stress, to change whatever was necessary to make life easier, worry-free and more prepared for unexpected circumstances.

I had to make more life changing decisions, but knew these changes were for what I wanted and needed.  After only three years living in my beautiful new condo on the beach, trying to rebuild life after the loss of my husband, I knew I had to move again.  The decision to move was to alleviate financial stress in case I got sick again. I wanted to maintain a lifestyle of living, but at half the expense. I sold the condo on the beach and I found a beautiful new townhome. The downsizing of expenses was to my comfort level without lowering my standard of living.

There are many things you can do to help yourself have a comfortable, calm and stress-free life, such as;

- **Financial**-Learn to earn, live below your means, have back up funds (enough to cover one year of bills) This gives you tremendous peace of mind. How to save the amount you need? Work, work, work. Give up spending thriftlessly.
- **Career/Job**-You must work at something you love, enjoy getting up to, with a feeling of purpose attached to your work. This is crucial for long-lasting happiness and overall well-being. Search within to find your passion, true path of direction, and purpose.
- **Positivity**-Let only positive people in your circle. Keep negativity out. Follow your own intuition on this. Your body is your gage. You will feel negativity when it's approaching or around you and it's up to you to avoid it and eliminate it. Surround yourself with people who make you happy, who enjoy the same things as you, and will support you in all areas of your life.
- **Control**-Take control of your own mind, your own life. Do what's best for YOU! Only you really know what you need and make sure you protect yourself for your own best interest. Say no, when you really want to say no…do not say yes and then wish you said no. Avoid the stress that comes with the seesaw act when dealing with others. Control your own life! Make your own path!
- **Health**-Maintain your health, eat properly, exercise moderately, socialize with friends and family, get your sleep, stay balanced.

To completely feel stress and worry free can take some time. But, working on the steps to get there is worth taking. Identify the things that stress you out and then begin to eliminate them. If you're asking yourself, what if it's a person? Well, YES, I have eliminated people from my life that were my stressors. Once I was engaged in my early twenties, and I just could not see myself living my life with someone who stressed me out all the time. So, I left. He wasn't the last either. I can't say this is easy, but it is necessary to reaching a peaceful, calm life. Choose your roads wisely. You do have a choice.

Facing change is never easy. But, remaining where you are and not feeling good is worse. This brings down your self-esteem, self-worth, confidence and outlook on life, a little each day. Until one day you are not you anymore.

Some of my affirmations I use are:

I have vowed never to be stressed by anyone ever.
I have chosen to live a more peaceful and calm life.
I say no when I mean no and say yes when I mean yes.
I do nothing that will cause me to be anxious, worry, or fearful.
I keep only positive people in my life and eliminate or detach from those who are not.
I live a purposeful life and have a purposeful career.
My faith and belief will remain strong.
I am willing to work hard for what I want and need.
I feel empowered and in control of my own life.

I live by what I teach. I live by these words. People always ask, how do you do this? Just start with one step and keep going.

FACING YOUR FEARS...

There are two kinds of fears.

- Fear in small amounts is fear that you can benefit from. This kind of (good) fear can make you work harder, focus more, educate yourself further and prepare you to not fail. This type of fear can cause you to be over prepared and confident, allowing you to reach your goals and succeed.

- Fear that is not beneficial causes anxiety, depression, and literally paralyzes you from moving forward. Keeping you from thinking clearly and making the right decisions for your life.

I coach many clients who have paralyzing fears. They seek answers on how to change their life; move ahead, leave a marriage/relationship, make a career change, enter a new relationship, and so on. I am the coach they look to and lean on to overcome the overwhelming fears that appear and reappear until they learn the process. If there is no one within your family/friends to help you with your life plan, seek outside professional help. The people I have coached and helped have turned their lives around. I mainly just guided them. They wanted the change, they just didn't know how to, and I organized it for them to stay on course to complete what they set out to do.

Did they have fears? YES. Did they feel overwhelmed at times? YES. Did they learn how to get through it and see their rewards? YES. Once you have removed fear, doubt, and gain confidence, strength, and motivation, you have started the uphill journey to getting your life back.

When in a state of fear, depression, and anxiety; you can feel like life is not worth living, like it's one big burden filled with too much pain and sorrow. I remember finding out some terrible things that my husband was involved with on the TV NEWS and Local newspapers. Shocking information, embarrassing, and it caused instant anxiety. Stress levels were extremely high and it would take years to get out of the mess. People were cruel and never asked for the real story.

One by one friends distant themselves from us. Even my own family judged him before knowing the facts. These were not easy days and life seemed to just "Stop". A distortion of time starts and how life was instantly changed in a day overwhelms you. One day peaceful, the next day full of chaos, distrust, fear, anxiety, and loss of the life you knew. This change happened in less than six hours. Arrests to bank accounts frozen, to needing a team of lawyers to defend oneself, was the beginning of the downfall.

Facing changes that involve the elimination of an entire career, severe financial loss, defamation of character, with no future to look forward to can be unbearable.

I remember praying a lot. I could not grasp what was happening and it all seemed like a bad movie. But, to get to the end of this horrible picture I had to keep going and watching it play out. It took time, but I recall *the steps I had to do*:

- ASSESS THE SITUATION with a clear mind and evaluate the steps you need to take to ease the circumstances.

**FINANCIALLY**

- SELL WHAT YOU NEED TO for legal expenses, downsize and eliminate bills. You must detach yourself from things and sell off what you really don't need.

- SPEND MINIMALLY – no dinning out, no shopping at all, no frills, just the basic needs.

- DO NOT BORROW from family or friends. This was difficult, but I stuck to it. Of course, my family offered to help us out. I always said no thank you. Bringing others into your situation can make you feel even worse. Find strength to find a way on your own.

**EMOTIONALLY**

- GET THROUGH THE EMOTIONS you are experiencing, but don't let it take too much of your time. Try to move through them and then move on. Spending too much time wallowing will keep you immobilized, feeling helpless, and will make it harder to adapt to the change. Everyone reacts differently and there are no right or wrong emotions. Allow time to heal.

- ALLOW PEOPLE TO SEE YOU, to know about the stress and pain. Allow them to help you through your change.

- ARTICULATE WHAT YOU NEED for receiving help. Most people do not know how to help someone going through a major life change. Especially those who haven't gone through any yet.

For them to help you, they need to be told exactly what you need from them. If they don't know, they'll probably not do anything.

- POSITIVE THOUGHTS will move you forward with hope that things will get better, easier, subside, and help with healing; body-mind and spirit.

- WHAT IS THE LESSON from this traumatic change? Ask yourself some questions; What am I supposed to learn? How do I see life now?

- HAVE FAITH and maintain your relationship with Divine Power (God) -take one day at a time. I have never lost faith, not even when I felt like life was not worth living. It WAS FAITH, belief and my relationship with (God), Angels, Spirit Guides that kept me strong, alive and hopeful. Never asking why? Only asking for strength and guidance to get through my difficult times.

EMOTIONAL responses are experienced whether you experienced a traumatic event, or have a family member or friend that has, or even witnessed or heard about the event on the news. People will experience all different kinds of symptoms.

- Extreme sadness (depression) and crying fits that seem to arise at any given time. I remember my friends making me laugh months after my husband died tragically, and then a fit of crying followed.

- Recurring dreams about the event.

- Feelings of disconnect with life, family friends.

- Constant change in emotions; guilt, shock, denial

- Mood changes include; irritability, anxiety

- Inability to focus, concentrate, do ordinary tasks

- Change in eating habits, not eating to overeating, eating poorly. Loss of appetite.

- Sleep patterns from insomnia to sleeping all the time.

- Withdrawal from society, friends, normal daily activities. Lack of interest.

- Increased consumption of alcohol, or other substances.

- Physical symptoms; aches/pains, fatigue, loss of energy, headaches.

When I was grieving and recovering from my traumatic loss, I was fortunate enough to have my mother watching over me and monitoring my symptoms. She was a bereavement counselor at that time and knew to watch if my symptoms persisted or worsened over time. They did. I went to my doctor seven times in a period of three months complaining of all sorts of aches and pains.

My mom talked me into going to the bereavement group at our church. I really did not want to go and thought who would understand what I am going through anyway. I also felt uneasy about being around people I don't know and crying in front of them. But, I went, and I am so thankful she pushed me into going. It helped me with doing something on a routine basis, it helped me with being around people, it helped me with my grief, I met others who were suffering the same, and we helped each other.

The bereavement group helped get the healing process started which I desperately needed.

ALWAYS seek medical and/or professional help if symptoms worsen. It may be necessary to seek medical, professional counseling, and clergy to assist you through the healing process.

When going through major life transition, you may find yourself viewing the world from a completely different perspective. It usually brings out greater resourcefulness and clarity. Those who have a strong survival sense will make do; those who are attached to their conveniences may not. When essentials are stripped away, we then can value the things that really matter, live a simpler and less stressed life.

Through the loss of my husband, my mother, a major life-threatening surgery and a major financial loss; I now understand and view life from a whole new perspective. I have detached myself from material things, even though I like them, they are not a necessity. I focus on my work, my Maltese dog, "Romeo", my family and friends. Each moment of my time is appreciated, valued and used wisely. I enjoy my family and friends to the fullest. I'm more giving. I'm more patient. I am aware of how short life really is, and in a moment, life can be gone, careers can be ended, and money can be lost. You must have faith and inner survival resources to rebuild, start new chapters of your life and create a new outlook.

*Facing difficult life transitions means;* facing your fears, overcoming trauma, and finding the courage to step back into life. This inner courage and the ability to move forward will help you to begin again. How do we get the courage we need? How do we restart life again? I found that staying extremely focused on what *I must do*; instead of dwelling on what has happened to me, has helped me adapt to my new life easier. Those who stay dwelling on the "why did this happen"- "why me"- "I don't know what do to" – have a much harder time reentering life and adapting to the new life set before them.

I truly believe when you overcome difficult times that you become a better, stronger you. I am a better version of me because of all my life transitions. I see things from a totally different perspective, with more clarity, compassion, empathy and wisdom. I also make better choices for myself, choices that are well thought out and overall are beneficial for my life and my work. It takes time to work through the layer of compounding issues and feel alive, productive, healthy and happy. Work at it, at your own pace. However long it takes. I can honestly say that it took me nearly ten years to fully adapt. We are beings in progress, growing, learning, adjusting and healing. We are all affected differently by our life experiences, so take your time to heal, but keep walking forward and look to your future.

# CHAPTER 2

## TAKE YOUR TIME

It can take years to heal. There is no timeline for healing from trauma. Coping with trauma and finding techniques that work for you is worth the trial and error. Treating the body-mind-and soul is necessary, and you may need multiple modalities to address these parts. Finding what will help you can be stressful at first, but when you do find it, it's like magic. It is worth trying things that you are resistant to, as I did with the bereavement group. I was highly resistant to going, and to make my mother happy, I went. It helped jumpstart me, I made friends within the group, and learned about the grief process from a spiritual point of view. It was a comfortable, peaceful environment that I looked forward to going to each week.

It can be frustrating in the beginning of the healing process. Family and friends all have opinions on what you should do and try. Whether seeking answers, closure, courage or strength; finding what works for you will require you to try all modalities that are available. You also must want to heal and put the past behind you. You must want to "feel normal" again however you can and move ahead. If you do not make a conscious effort to free yourself, you will remain "stuck" in the mind, in life; to only find yourself years later in the same mindset.

Having support at home, work, from family, friends, and from therapists/counselors is crucial to healing. Once you find the support and therapy needed, stick to it and follow through with the sessions. It can *feel like* nothing is working at the onset, but it is. I get asked often, "How long do you think it will be before I feel better?" Healing time is different for each individual and circumstance. Do not put a time frame on healing. Allow the healing process to evolve each day. I believe once a person decides to commit to healing, releasing emotions, forgiving, and seeking treatments that they are comfortable with, is when the healing process begins. Consistency of healing work is important.

Committing to the healing process:

- Affirms your will to survive surviving
- Drives your will and desire for freedom
- Empowers you to take control of your life once again
- Assists in removing fear from change
- Confirms to yourself that you want to move past the trauma

Individuals will heal from trauma at a different pace. Some have more resiliency than others. Some have more supportive resources. Some need time, a lot of time. It doesn't matter the length of time. It matters that you start the healing process. Give yourself permission to take the time you need and be patient with yourself.

You will have your ups and downs with emotions. Trigger days such as holidays, birthdays, special events and other memorable days can start a low cycle of negative thoughts. During these low cycles you may feel;

- Life has no meaning
- A lack of sense of direction
- Uninterested in life
- Lost with no goals
- Life is not worth living

- Doubtful about future
- You cannot handle life under present circumstances
- Like giving up
- Lack of clarity and focus
- Stuck
- Fearful of living life

Healing can begin when you become annoyed with these feelings. I remember not wanting to cry that deep cry anymore. It was so painful, I felt like I would have a heart attack. I said that day, "I'm sorry, I cannot cry for you like this anymore. It doesn't mean I don't love you or miss you, I just can't cry like this anymore." That was so releasing and freeing. I cried after that, but not the deep grief painful cry. That was finished! The mind is so powerful. You can direct it thoughts that better suit you, but only when you are ready.

I also remember while in a low cycle talking to myself. Saying that I didn't want to remain years in this negative place. It was so heavy and draining. I kept thinking that I have so many years left to journey on earth and it will be too difficult to stay in the low cycle and I MUST get out of it. That was the beginning of the turn-around for me. I knew I had to figure it out, but how?

When I was grief-stricken and in shock from my husband's sudden passing from an accident, I was immediately thrown into;

- Disbelief
- Shock & Confusion
- Depression & Intense Sadness

I entered the low cycle in a minute. This loss was devastating. He was my soulmate, my love, my best friend and looked forward to growing old together. The loss of him triggered secondary losses such as;

LOSS OF:
- Life-style
- Work
- Friends
- Home
- Income

My mother was a crucial support during this time and for directing me towards the path to heal. She got me out of the house, made sure I ate healthy and at least one meal a day. She talked me into going to a bereavement program at our local church. These beginning steps may be too difficult to do on your own, but if you do not have that strong support you must try to.

A year went by and my mother, sister and her husband and daughter moved to Arizona to be with my other sister. I was still in shock over the current situation and now losing my family to a move across country. Although my brother remained in Manhattan and was so thankful for, I could not bear this loss. It was truly devasting to now lose my mom and sister who were also my best friends! We did everything together. My husband and my mother were best friends…we all were always together. My mom lived one block away. The feeling of abandonment I suffered was nothing I have ever experienced before. I thought to move out there also, but just couldn't at that time. I suffered quietly while they began a new life.

A few years later, my mother got ill and passed away. I still was grieving the loss of my husband, moving myself to

New Jersey, leaving my business, trying to start new, and then my mother passes away. I entered the low cycle again. I just could not find peace, happiness, and felt lost in life.

Grief, stress, deep depression made me sick. I became ill now. This for me was the final eye-opening catalyst of awareness. I was told I had ovarian cancer stage 3 and went to Sloan Kettering in Manhattan.
My faith was super strong and was the only comfort I had. I prayed even harder now, for some kind-of miracle, relief. I was humbled by this and never asked why me. I asked please help me. I was preparing for surgery and *witnessed a visit by Jesus and I felt white light inside me.* When I awoke from surgery, the Doctor said he could not find a stitch cancer in me. He said he searched and even went to pathology to review for himself. He kept me open for another hour to search everywhere. I received my miracle of health. This changed my life forever!

Having witnessed these miracles from GOD/JESUS, from REIKI (A spiritual healing) has had a profound effect on my life. I have always been extremely spiritual, but this awakening brought me to another level. I now had to re-arrange my life and learn more, become more, and help others.

I had *time* to see life with new eyes. I was given a second chance, a chance to change, heal, find new purpose, create a new life and begin the steps to start over. I was clean-slated; and it was now time to follow higher guidance and new direction. My FAITH had the biggest role in my healing process. My senses seemed more acute, my inner guidance stronger, louder and the abound presence of GOD, Angels and my Spirit Guides were felt, heard and seen unlike I've experienced before as an Intuitive. My soul needed to feel healthy, strong, passionate and purposeful.

When shattered by life difficulties, it can seem overwhelming to get through. The thought of trying to adapt can seem impossible. I began to study myself through my grief and compounding losses. I needed to answer some serious questions.

Questions I asked were:

1. What do I need to do to calm my mind?
2. What does my body need?
3. Where will I be happiest living and starting a new life alone?
4. Are my finances in order?
5. What do I see myself doing in the future, becoming, enjoying?
6. Will I surrender to GOD and follow higher guidance and direction?

I answered these questions. It was helpful to begin structuring life again. I chose to pray more and ask for guidance, signs, a shove in the direction I was supposed to take. Divine intervention is powerful…! Worth following and being surprised with the outcome. During this time, I was visited by an Angel one night and was told to write my book. Since I decided to listen to every sign and message, I wrote my first book; "It's Time To Believe" in Angels, Spirit Guides and Yourself. Then I wrote my second book; "Automatic Trance Writing" the Power to Receive Messages from Beyond. I never thought of writing any books. Divine intervention was abundant. I promised to listen and follow. I am now an Author. I was told I would write five books. This one is the third. I have no idea what the other two will be, but I am sure GOD knows.

This was the time to take whatever time is needed to rebuild and start new paths. I just knew I had to start my new career in alternative medicine- Reiki, Hypnotherapy and EMT/EMDR. I received proper training and certification over the next few years and now I am a Master Hypnotherapist (Clinical & Spiritual), Reiki Master, and trained in EMDR.

Reiki is a technique called palm healing or hands-on healing through which a "universal energy" is transferred from the practitioner to the patient for emotional or physical healing. This is a highly spiritual modality and I have witnessed many healings. I use prayer and guided mediation during a Reiki session, and I also offer hypnotic reiki.

Hypnotherapy and EMDR has significantly helped me with trauma related issues and overcoming the emotions attached to the trauma. After these sessions, I felt free to move forward with a positive mindset.

TAKE YOUR TIME in redirecting your life. Write your own questions down that need answered. Evaluate and study yourself. What steps do you have to start to begin your healing journey? You have choices that can change your life and help the healing process.

You first must want to make any necessary change to heal and start over.

Then a new life begins.

# CHAPTER 3

## NEED A BREAKTHROUGH

Breakthroughs are necessary for moving ahead. You may experience a breakthrough, but the "epiphany" breakthrough visits like a hammer on your head. This breakthrough is needed for getting your life back.
Praying for help is a great start, but you will have to do the work. I believe that *Divine Intervention* will occur if you allow it and open yourself to being spiritually molded to start a new journey as a new you.

What is Divine Intervention?

**Divine intervention** is the interference of a deity in human life, popularly extended to any miraculous-seeming turn of events.
A miracle or act of god (or gods) that causes something good to happen or stops something bad from happening.

Being a strong believer, a true spiritualist, will allow GOD to ask you to do certain things. You may be fearful or wondering how you will do what is asked of Him, (as I was when they told me to write a book), but whatever the message, begin the steps of doing what is asked. I ONLY live by this and it has taken me on many new and exciting journeys I never dreamed of. It becomes one surprise/miracle after another every day.

**Spiritual breakthroughs** create a sense of well-being, peace, empowerment and hope for the future. Relying on GOD and yourself to focus on healing and creating new paths. That "ah-ha" moment of realization of reality and what is *needed to do*. This is the time to start focusing your energy on answers and provide yourself with attainable steps.

I remember all my breakthroughs. One strong one was when I was sitting home alone recovering after surgery. It hit me like a thunderbolt. The message I heard was…You are on your own now, no-one but you can get you through this. It was a terrible awakening but very much needed. I really didn't have family members to count on, nor a partner, and I certainly didn't want to bother any friends. So, yes, I was on my own. Years of having my husband and my mother and father to count on and lean on were gone. My support team was gone.

This was a turning point in my life, for my healing, for getting my life in order the way I needed it. The way GOD wanted it. I did not ask advice from anyone. I prayed for answers, signs, messages and divine guidance. I received all my answers. With a spiritual breakthrough, comes accountability. Higher power steers you, but you must follow and walk the path. I was accountable not only to myself but to GOD. You must do the work. You may not like what you need to do, but your soul knows you must.

Being a master hypnotherapist and reiki master, I learned to develop and master controlling my thoughts and emotions. Mastering fear doesn't mean there isn't fear, mastering the ability to control levels of anxiety and even remove it has been highly beneficial. To be able turn negative thoughts, emotions and behaviors into new positive ways has also changed my life.

A breakthrough requires you to truly evaluate yourself, your life, the direction you are going in and an urge to start with a clean-slate. Breakthroughs are life-changing events.

You are entering a new phase, walking a new path and usually with a new set of people.

Spiritually you may be tested or prepared by God before a breakthrough. I have been prepared many times prior to a breakthrough not realizing at the time, but later understanding how beneficial it was to experience the test and preparation.

Signs of a breakthrough or shift occurring may include:

- A strong desire to understand life on a deeper level
- Freeing yourself from materialism
- Urge to feel more purposeful with work, family and all aspects of self
- Self-transformation that is noticeable to others by actions and behaviors
- Disassociating with life, not wanting to participate but sit back as a spectator
- Wanting to be healthier and care for the body more
- Needing to be alone more to work on oneself
- A heightened awareness of time and the value of time
- Accepting universal laws, guidance from higher power, feeling calm and patient
- A strong desire to be more spiritual, connect on a deeper level with your soul, with nature, with God
- Wanting to be released from society's rules – living life just as you wish

Are you needing a change? A real breakthrough? You won't find it amongst your family and friends. Nor will it come from therapists and doctors. It comes from within. It comes from divine intervention, God, the universe, Angels and Spirit Guides. It comes from your soul. You will be able to "feel" something pulling you, speaking to your inner self that will guide you and show you the way.

Pray with FAITH and DILIGENCE. Pray to be guided and sent what you need to move forward, reach goals and dreams. Divine intervention leads you to places you never thought of. It will feel surreal and magical. After I wrote my first book, I felt this way. I couldn't remember the process, nor could I believe where I ended up. As I stood in Barnes & Noble for a book debut, in front of over a hundred people, I was in awe. I was in awe of what God, higher power provided for me. It felt like a dream.

How did I get here? DIVINE INTERVENTION! This was a breakthrough for me. I had new paths to take and more books to write. The doors of abundance were open. I opened my life to God, to the power of the universe and it has been unbelievable since then.
Pray patiently. Sometimes prayers are answered quickly and other times one must be patient. You receive what and when you need something at exactly the right moment. Higher power knows what is best for us before we do. We are to complete steps along the way and wait for the spiritual breakthrough. So be patient and stay strong in faith. Sit back and patiently wait for you will be rewarded.

I feel it is extremely important to point out that we are given free will. You will be sent what you need and guided always on the promising path. You have a choice. Many pass up opportunities, ignore those inner voices that are guiding them, only to find they are still in the same place feeling as if the prayers were not answered.

CHOOSING to listen, follow, overcome fear, try a new way, a new path, a new career will open your world. Allow the breakthrough to happen! Enjoy the surprises along the way. Look forward to life and experiencing more than you ever imagined.

You may be battling for a breakthrough. Unseen negative spiritual forces will try to divert you. You must maintain faith and belief and fight against frustration, discouragement, doubt and weariness. Never give up nor never give in to the dark spiritual forces!

BIBLE VERSES for Spiritual Breakthroughs

1 Corinthians 10:13
No temptation has overtaken you that is not common to man. God is faithful, and he will not let you be tempted beyond your ability, but with the temptation he will also provide the way of escape, that you may be able to endure it.

Proverbs 4:25-27
Let your eyes look directly forward, and your gaze be straight before you. Ponder the path of your feet; then all your ways will be sure. Do not swerve to the right or to the left; turn your foot away from evil.

Ephesians 6:12
For we do not wrestle against flesh and blood, but against the rulers, against the authorities, against the cosmic powers over this present darkness, against the spiritual forces of evil in the heavenly places.

### Isaiah 43:19
Behold, I am doing a new thing; now it springs forth, do you not perceive it? I will make a way in the wilderness and rivers in the desert.

### Galatians 1:10
For am I now seeking the approval of man, or of God? Or am I trying to please man? If I were still trying to please man, I would not be a servant of Christ.

### Romans 12:1-21
I appeal to you therefore, brothers, by the mercies of God, to present your bodies as a living sacrifice, holy and acceptable to God, which is your spiritual worship. Do not be conformed to this world, but be transformed by the renewal of your mind, that by testing you may discern what is the will of God, what is good and acceptable and perfect. For by the grace given to me I say to everyone among you not to think of himself more highly than he ought to think, but to think with sober judgment, each according to the measure of faith that God has assigned. For as in one body we have many members, and the members do not all have the same function, so we, though many, are one body in Christ, and individually members one of another. ...

### Jeremiah 29:11
For I know the plans I have for you, declares the LORD, plans for welfare and not for evil, to give you a future and a hope.

### Philippians 4:19
And my God will supply every need of yours according to his riches in glory in Christ Jesus.

## 2 Chronicles 7:14

If my people who are called by my name humble themselves and pray and seek my face and turn from their wicked ways, then I will hear from heaven and will forgive their sin and heal their land.

## Psalm 37:4

Delight yourself in the LORD, and he will give you the desires of your heart.

## 1 John 2:15-17

Do not love the world or the things in the world. If anyone loves the world, the love of the Father is not in him. For all that is in the world—the desires of the flesh and the desires of the eyes and pride in possessions—is not from the Father but is from the world. And the world is passing away along with its desires, but whoever does the will of God abides forever.

## Galatians 5:19-21

Now the works of the flesh are evident: sexual immorality, impurity, sensuality, idolatry, sorcery, enmity, strife, jealousy, fits of anger, rivalries, dissensions, divisions, envy, drunkenness, orgies, and things like these. I warn you, as I warned you before, that those who do such things will not inherit the kingdom of God.

## John 14:6

Jesus said to him, "I am the way, and the truth, and the life. No one comes to the Father except through me.

A spiritual breakthrough will alter the direction of your life. It's a detour that takes you on a new road that seems to be navigated by higher power. Once on this new road, a feeling of peace and that everything will be alright encompasses you.

# CHAPTER 4

## THERAPY FOR HEALING

To begin healing when going through a difficult period can be frustrating. Family and friends all have opinions on what you should do, can either be helpful or make you more frustrated and confused.

Whether seeking answers, closure, courage or strength, finding what works for you will require you to try all that's available. I found the spiritual-holistic path of EMDR, Hypnosis and Reiki was highly beneficial. So much that I became a Master Hypnotherapist (Clinical & Spiritual), EMDR trained and a Reiki Master. I had to reach into my subconscious and soul to overcome internal thoughts and processes.

For any healing to occur, you must first want to be healed, to feel better, to let go and begin life once again. If you do not want this, you will not heal. You will remain "stuck" in the mind, in actions and behaviors, and in all areas of life. To find yourself months or years later still in the same space, not gaining any happiness, and remaining in the cycle of negative thought.

When trying to get through grief, divorce, relationship break-ups, financial duress and illness, it can feel as if life has no purpose or meaning. It can take the most positive person to all-time low vibration negative space and be brutally difficult to rise back. This process I have been through. It has been a journey that has been brutal and powerful at the same time. Prayer, Reiki, EMDR and Hypnotherapy were the most powerful tools to getting my life back.

## PRAYER

First and foremost, I ALWAYS turn to prayer. Never giving up faith in what is supposed to be and what will be. I have witnessed miracles for myself and others over the years and prayer has never let me down. When you turn to (GOD) higher power for healing, you must surrender and allow HIS Holy Spirit work in and through you. I was facing a serious illness and was told I had 3-5 years left to live. Rushed to Sloan in Manhattan, I surely thought I would not have long to live. I prayed for a miracle. I prayed for everyone else that was there. I never asked WHY ME? I am nobody special to not get cancer, I just prayed for help. REIKI was given to me and felt a white ball of light zooming all around inside me. It was a strange and beautiful feeling and I still did not know what the outcome would be. Before surgery I deeply prayed and I saw a vision of Jesus, my husband, my mother and knew Spirit was with me.

Upon awakening, the Surgeon stated I was extremely lucky and won the lottery. Not a stitch of cancer. This changed my life. *Prayer has been the most powerful tool and my faith never waivers.* I did not know I would be healed and was truly amazed and grateful for the blessing of health. All matters after this experience seemed unimportant. My perspective on life has changed. There is now nothing to stress about or worry about. Daily life is peaceful and calm. I now focus my work on holistic and spiritual healing, my art and music. Life is simpler. **An "awakening" has occurred.**

### What is an awakening?

An awakening is when one transcends to higher consciousness and awareness, which brings one peace and calmness. A feeling of just "knowing" all will be ok. A shift in consciousness occurs where you now perceive life differently than before. You are now in a state of being spiritually aware at a higher level.

# SIGNS OF A SPIRITUAL AWAKENING

- **Higher Perception of the World**
  Perceive the world different than others. As if you had a pair of new eyes. Seeing things others would take for granted. Amazed and captivated by all living things. Plant life, Animals, the Sea, the sky and universe. The world can seem brighter, sharper and a oneness with all life overwhelms you. An increase of sensitivity to the world around you with a new appreciation for the simple things in life.

- **TIME Shift**
  A shift in consciousness occurs about time. Being more in the present and appreciating and living in the moment. This time shift allows one to not dwell on the past or daydream about the future, which then allows time to expand. You seem to now have more time to do what is needed in the present. Your focus on the present increases and you seem to get more and more accomplished. Time seems to disappear.

- **DIVINE PRESENCE and SPIRITUAL SOURCE**
  A connection with GOD, Angels, Spirit Guides and Spiritual energy seems to be everywhere. This true connection creates protection, peace, love and

where all things are manifested.  You may witness miracles and feel completely in awe of this power that you now have connected with and access to. Once open to spiritual source and divine presence your life changes and you may find yourself living a new way of life, reaching dreams you never thought of, and finally realizing that divine intervention guided you the entire way. All is connected as a oneness of energy with a sense that all is ok and will remain ok.

- **THE REBIRTH**
  After an awakening if gradual you will a change of shift occur slowly in your thoughts and actions. But you do realize now you are just not the same.  A sudden awakening happens in an instant and you will be able to remember that exact moment precisely.  The shift in you occurs immediately, as if the light bulb went off in your head. The old self is put to rest and this new self emerges. It's as if you are spiritual clay be remolded and you now are a completely different person. It is noticeable amongst those closest to you and they can see the change. They may make statements such as; You're not the same person or you seem different.  Rightly so, you are not the same as you were before the awakening.

A new self emerges, the inner life shift is profound. There is a sense of having a rebirth, a spiritual cleanse, as if becoming an entirely new person.

- **PEACFUL INNER QUIETNESS**
  The mind now seems peaceful and quiet. Open to divine guidance and direction, able to focus on the present and with clarity. Thoughts that once caused

repetitive or negative thinking are gone. A clearing occurs and the mind is now free. You seem to be clear of inner chatter and the mind is completely clear. You feel lighter, calmer, peaceful and open to receive clear guidance. A calmness of the mind makes room for growth and preparation for the new life, new path begins.

- **EMPATHY**
  A higher empathy and awareness for all life occurs. A need to help others and care for the well-being of all life is abound. You may once have stepped on a worm or insect and now walk around it. Connecting with all life energy and feeling more love and compassion for all existence.

- **SENSE of WELL-BEING**
  You feel different and it is noticeable to not only you but others.
  You now have an extreme sense of contentment, less prone to negativity, boredom and loneliness. You have mastered your thoughts to ONLY think positive and remove all negative thinking. Freeing you from worry and mind clutter. A feeling of peace, bliss and gratitude engulfs you. Happy with the simple things. Also freeing oneself from materialism. Enjoying what you have, but not attached to it anymore. Wanting and needing less. A feeling of balance of mind, body and spirit.

- **OUTLOOK on LIFE**
  You now seem to have a *heightened awareness of actions and choices*, that not only affect yourself but others. Caring for all life and aware of all needs. Choosing purpose and fulfilment over anything else. Balancing what you need and creating the life

you want. A feeling of openness to universal ways and higher power (GOD) to guide you and lead you in the direction for your higher good. There is a feeling of calmness and all will be ok.

- **GRATEFULNESS and APPRECIATION**
  You now feel grateful for what you have than thinking about what you don't have. Putting a higher value on health, free from worry and an overall sense of well-being. Have gratitude and appreciation for everything and is noticeable to oneself. Thankful for even the smallest things.

There is strong disconnect from ordinary daily life. Viewing life differently with a heightened sense of time creates a surge of energy, reaching your higher potential, balance and growth. Now peaceful and calm, balanced and pacing yourself wisely. Choosing new paths without fear or worry. Creating a positive environment and mind, making clear decisions and looking forward to life ahead knowing it all will be ok.

A SPIRIUTAL AWAKENING is WONDERFUL & LIFE CHANGING!
Whenever and however it occurs embrace it!

When life seems to be breaking you down, your hope, confidence, ability to move forward and so on…where do you turn? This is a very important question.

- Are you turning to family or friends that are not really helping you?
- Are you listening to the wrong people?

- Are you looking for the answer you want to hear?
- Did you lose faith? Abandon GOD? Blame GOD?
- Are you relying on someone else to fix the situation? Who?

*My first place to turn to is prayer.* That has worked for me beyond belief. I have witnessed miracle after miracle and cannot explain how true belief and prayer has opened so many pathways. The more I prayed and listened, the more I received. The truthful answers are always within. Family and friends have witnessed my blessings and healings. I ask everyone who is in need to at least try praying, connect with their spirituality, begin soul searching and ask for guidance from Higher Power. Leave yourself free and open to wherever you are guided.

The power of the universe, higher power, is available for everyone to use. It must be a true spiritual belief and connection. You also must be patient and wait for the gift of receiving what you need. I get prayers answered sometime within hours, days and some months to years. The proper timing for everything is not what we think it is, it is what higher power knows it is. Through a spiritual awakening you understand this and accept it. No need to fight the timing of things or worry. You now know to just let things happen as they are supposed to. I look at it now as waiting for the gift. *When it is time to get it, I will.*

During the recovery years (yes, it can take years) there are helpful physical practices that can help calm the brain when needed. Physical exercise, yoga, dance, somatic therapy, breath and body awareness. It helps to learn and do something physical that calms and distracts the mind.

Practice internal talking with yourself. Try to reframe your thoughts and redirect your thoughts to thinking more positive thoughts. This requires mastering your own mind and yes, we do have the ability to do so, with practice. Traumatic memories are stored in the part of the brain responsible for our emotions. Therefor; when a traumatic memory resurfaces, the emotions and physical functions are stimulated, causing the traumatic event to "feel like" it's happening in the present. It is most beneficial to practice reframing and learn breathing techniques that can help calm you when you need.

Working and feeling purposeful is highly beneficial for moving through a difficult period. Keeping busy, active, feeling connected and staying social will keep you grounded. Finding new work, doing something that gives you a reason or purpose to live life is worth finding. After the loss of my husband, I had another awakening. I just knew I had to move. I didn't want to move, I just knew I had to. I picked up and left a career behind, our home was sold, and to New Jersey from New York I went. Beginning life where I wanted it to be. Near the beach.

With each awakening, you may learn something different and move to a higher spiritual level. I learned that I could start life anywhere and I had a choice. I learned that the inner knowing can be quite strong and something you should listen to and follow. The soul speaks during an awakening and difficult times, you just need to listen it.

Holistic Therapies that helped me were:

**REIKI**

What is REIKI? (Life Force Energy)

**Reiki** is an energy healing practice that is usually done by placing the hands in a series of positions over or slightly above the body. **Reiki** promotes healing by activating the relaxation response and helping the body to balance itself from a very deep level. Reiki is a healing technique based on the principle that the therapist can channel energy into the client to activate the natural healing processes of the patient's body and restore physical and emotional well-being. Reiki has an energy of its own providing healing, insight, inner-transformation and spiritual connection.

Reiki is used as a supplemental to medicine not to be used solely for serious medical issues. It is an ancient practice and has proven outcomes for healing, even miracles. I have received Reiki and witnessed my own miracle first-hand. Healing white light was sent to me before my surgery and even though a team of doctors stated devastating news of ovarian cancer, I was healed. Not a stitch of cancer. They were amazed also, stating I won the lottery. I knew I was healed and blessed.

The energy within and around us needs balancing, healing, cleansing and calming. Look for a Reiki Master to try this wonderful spiritual modality and keep an open heart and mind. Enjoy the peacefulness and positive energy flow from each session.

## HYPNOTHERAPY

What is HYPNOTHERAPY?

Hypnotherapy is guided hypnosis, or a trance-like state of focus and concentration achieved with the help of a certified clinical hypnotherapist. This trance-like state is similar to being completely absorbed in a book, movie, music, or even one's own thoughts or meditations. In this state, one can turn their attention completely inward to find and *utilize the natural resources deep within themselves* that can help them make changes or regain control in certain areas of their life. It is a reframing of the way one thinks.

Hypnotherapy is a modality for inner work. It is important to do inner work in general and more importantly when going through a difficult period.  Guided Hypnosis assists with changing thought patterns from negative to positive, from despair to hope, from self-defeat to self-assurance and confidence and much more.

There are numerous ways to reprogram thought patterns and behaviors.

**Neuro-Linguistic Programming -NLP**
Inner communication is a strong suit of **Neuro-Linguistic Programming**, which was originally known as the study of the structure of subjective experience. It means that **NLP** breaks down what's going on in your conscious and sub-conscious mind so that you can **do** something constructive and positive with it.

**NLP** alone is not necessarily **hypnosis**.

NLP has no formal induction. It doesn't use the same tools and techniques as **hypnosis**, but because both your conscious mind and unconscious mind are involved it is modeled under hypnosis techniques and can be utilized with hypnosis.

The difference between hypnosis and NLP are that in **hypnosis** all the commands are given when the client is in trance and the subconscious mind is at the forefront. Whereas in **NLP**, the client is fully conscious and works on the techniques while the **NLP** practitioner guides the session.

Then there is a powerful modality used today for healing & processing trauma and disturbing life experiences. There are many books about EMDR techniques explaining the full process. This overview is shortened and to the point.

**EMDR** (Eye Movement Desensitization and Reprocessing) is a psychotherapy that enables people to heal from the symptoms and emotional distress that are the result of disturbing life experiences. **EMDR** therapy shows that the mind can in fact heal from psychological trauma.

Eye-Movement Therapy helps with the processing of trauma and the emotions attached with it. EMDR does not remove the images or memories of the experience, but removes the emotions attached to it. This means that once the process is complete you should be able to talk about the event without emotional interference.

## Mind and body practices

Mind-body techniques strengthen the communication between your mind and your body. CAM practitioners say these two systems must be in harmony for you to stay healthy. Examples of mind-body connection techniques include hypnosis, reiki, meditation, prayer, relaxation and art therapies.

Manipulation and body-based practices use human touch to move or manipulate a specific part of your body. They include chiropractic and osteopathic manipulation and massage.

Some CAM practitioners believe an invisible energy force flows through your body, and when this energy flow is blocked or unbalanced, you can become sick. Different traditions call this energy by different names, such as chi, prana and life force. The goal of these therapies is to unblock or re-balance your energy force. Energy therapies include qi gong, healing touch and reiki.

The terms "alternative," "complementary," and "lifestyle" medicine are used to describe many kinds of products, practices, and treatments that are not part of standard or traditional medicine.

- Alternative therapy refers to non-standard treatment used *in place of* standard treatment.
- Complementary therapy usually means methods used *along with* standard treatment.
- Lifestyle medicine is a newer field that describes its approach as preventing and treating illness through healthy eating, physical activity, and other healthy behaviors without the use of medicine.

I personally feel Complementary therapy is the correct route to healing. If I did not get to Sloan for proper medical care I probably would not be here today. Did I receive Reiki and a miracle along with traditional medicine…YES!

*When dealing with a serious medical issue,* I advise seeking proper medical treatment and speaking with your primary health care provider prior to using holistic therapies as adjuvant therapy.

Most CAM (Complementary and Alternative Medicine) therapies have a holistic approach which believes that health flows from the harmonious balance of our physical, psychological and spiritual states. A disruption in any of these can impact one or the other and disrupt the healing process.

**Complementary and alternative medicine (CAM) can include the following:**

- acupuncture,
- Alexander technique,
- aromatherapy,
- Ayurveda (Ayurvedic medicine),
- biofeedback,
- chiropractic medicine,
- diet therapy,
- herbalism,
- holistic nursing,
- homeopathy,
- hypnosis,
- massage therapy,
- meditation,
- naturopathy,
- nutritional therapy,
- osteopathic manipulative therapy (OMT),
- Qi gong (internal and external Qiging),

- reflexology,

- Reiki,

- spiritual healing,

- Tai Chi,

- traditional Chinese Medicine (TCM), and

- yoga.

**Whatever therapy you are drawn to for healing,** do what feels best and is helping you maintain mind, body, spirit balance along with keeping you feeling calm and peaceful.

*(Remember that CAM therapies are NOT a replacement for medical treatment and seeking professional medical care when you need is an absolute must.)*

### Healing Power of PETS

I have always loved animals and all life, but never realized the amazing healing powers they contribute when going through a difficult period. I can say my dog "Romeo" saved my life. Having to be responsible for another life helped me regain my own life. Interacting with a pet is great therapy. Walking with them allows you to move and exercise more when you may feel like not moving at all. Giving and receiving love, cuddling with them is great comfort and a stress reliever. They are simply an effective form of comfort while giving a sense of purpose.

I remember the moment of having "Romeo" my Maltese in my hands. It was instant love. My entire life changed upon his arrival. I was grieving multiple losses, dealing with a major health issue and surgery and a relationship breakup. This beautiful puppy was now MY responsibility and the changes were profound.

- I went out more, by walking him, going to dog parks and pet friendly establishments. Strolling the boardwalk along the ocean.
- I interacted socially more having him with me.
- I exercised now with longer walks as he grew older.
- I educated myself and went to grooming school and received my Groomer's Certification.
  Also, enrolled in the local dog therapy program and Romeo became a therapy dog too.

The responsibility of caring for another life removes you from the pain of your own life and helps your emotional state incredibly. One can become very attached to their pet(s) as I have, and life changes around their needs.

"Romeo" grounded me, kept me from being irresponsible, motivated me to learn about the breed and their needs. He is a family member and cares for me just the same…they sense what you need also.

It was difficult having a puppy on my own, but I had friends to help. It was worth the work to train him and rearrange my work and life for him. I enjoy being home with him, working from home, and having the cutest little buddy anyone could ever ask for.

My clients enjoy him during their reiki and hypnosis sessions as he lays right next to them. They fill a void, they

give unconditional love, and simply make you happier.
They are a great distraction from whatever you may be
dealing with and allows you to move past issues in your
own life a little easier.

So, whether you are dealing with grief, illness, depression,
anxiety etc., a pet can help you through. If you can't have a
pet, you can volunteer at a shelter, or dog/cat sit for a
friend. I have many friends who take Romeo and enjoy
him.

Studies show that interacting with animals (even fish!)
helps lower blood pressure, reduce anxiety, and decrease
depression. Scientist also observe that interacting with
animals increases levels of the hormone oxytocin. Oxytocin
has a number of important effects on the body. It slows a
person's heart rate and breathing, reduces blood pressure,
and inhibits the production of stress hormones. All of these
changes help create a sense of calm and comfort.

This healing can be emotional as well as physical, as
oxytocin makes us feel happy, encourages trust,
and promotes bonding. This helps explain why we literally
fall in love with our pets.
At the same time, pets offer us their unconditional love—
and yes, even empathy—in return. After a cancer diagnosis
and during treatment, pets don't judge or try to give advice.

Pets are just there when you need them, for emotional,
physical and social benefits. They show affection,  provide
companionship, and offer great comfort.

# CHAPTER 5

## YOU HAVE A CHOICE

Making choices in life in general can be difficult and even more difficult when going through a life transition. The circle of questions swirling around in the mind can confuse you even more. I found that slowing yourself down to THINK before making life changes brings clarity to the situation. You first must want to *choose* a positive path to move forward on and then *choose* how to get there.

SPIRITUALLY YOU CAN CHOOSE TO:

- Pray
- Join spiritual group
- Believe in God, Angels and yourself
- Be courageous
- Stay faithful

FINANCIALLY YOU CAN CHOOSE TO:

- Change career/job
- Work more/second job
- Downsize bills
- Eliminate debt
- Continue education for stability of work/money and purpose

EMOTIONALLY YOU CAN CHOOSE TO:

- Stay calm & peaceful
- Practice mind-body-spiritual modalities
- Keep positivity around you and remove all negativity

- Stop worrying and enjoy the present

The most powerful tool you have is your MIND! A new way of thinking brings new perspective and outcomes. When you decide to act…growth begins. It may not be easy, but it is where it begins. Recondition your mind to think positive and create the future you want. There will be plenty of choices, but your inner soul knows the true path. Every decision you make is important.

Some choices are:

- Give up
- Stay the same
- Reach for desires
- Keep going forward

Once you decide to go forward, start new, create a new path and a new life it all brings about an inner peace and direction. The gray zone leads nowhere. Strong decisions force strong actions.

A healthy mind is peaceful, worry-free, positive thinking, realistic and clear of interference. A healthy *Spiritual Mind* releases care and worries to GOD -Higher Power-Universe and receives guidance that redirects one's life. Freeing the mind from unnecessary worry.

Choosing to have a healthy mind is key to healing and moving forward. I remember praying for my mind to return to normal. I wanted a clear and healthy mind and I knew I could not make the best decisions unless my mind was clear. I waited patiently for my mind to calm down and then I could think of options for moving forward.

Choosing a spiritual path while going through my own difficult periods seemed to ease the burdens. I was sent signs and guidance through divine intervention that redirected my life. It took me where I never even thought of, such as; being an Author. I rely on divine intervention. It has never steered me wrong. I have only attained and reached more through this spiritual connection. Spiritual surprises occur daily. Amazing changes can occur once you choose a spiritual path and maintain faith.

A spiritual path takes you on a different road.

You now choose:

… peace and tranquility over drama and chaos.
… to accept the nature of life and release worry and fear
… to be healthy and happy
… to belong and at times to be alone
… to see life simpler and grateful for life itself
… faith and commitment to GOD with full trust

Finding your spiritual path is a very personal journey. It starts from within. The soul speaks to us all the time. Most don't listen. Once open to your spiritual path the soul speaks louder. Follow the inner guidance and witness the miracles of growth and change. Living a true spiritual journey requires one to find purpose and fulfillment. To realize we have a higher self that needs to be nourished and brought out.
*Prayer and spirituality for myself has been the strongest influence for moving forward and regaining my life back. I trust this more than anything else.* Of course, putting in the work along way is required, but you will be guided.

You must find strength to act upon the decisions you deep down know you should do. Many people know what they should do but fear of change or lack of courage paralyzes them. They find themselves "stuck" in a situation that within due time can find even more intolerable. I have family and friends that could not find the courage to do what was needed of them to create a better life, a different life, a new life. Finding themselves unhappy, unfulfilled, in the same place or worse, only to say they made bad choices and missed opportunities to better their life. REGRETS now begin and looking back creates more unhappiness.

CHOOSE wisely during life transitions. Take a moment to really think about what you need to do to make life better, easier, peaceful and purposeful. *Life is a series of choices that not only create your current situation and experience but are connective choices in creating your future.* The choices you have made up until the present have created your life. You can make better and wiser choices as you learn the process of spiritual growth and transition.
The conscious mind is your critical mind which can block you from moving ahead. Connecting with higher power, the universe and tapping into these sources allows one to spiritually grow and be awakened and enlightened.

Spend some time in meditation and prayer. Ask for guidance and direction. You will see the wonderment of the universe and the gifts that will be sent. It will be up to you to accept them.
Whatever choices you make, believe in your choices, believe you are guided and directed for your higher good. Believe you can and will change things around and begin the steps necessary. One-step at a time.

**Remember there is always a choice...Great quotes to ponder:**

Happiness is not something ready-made. It comes from your own actions.

-Dalai Lama

Let a series of happy thoughts run through your mind. They will show on your face.

-Unknown

Experience tells you what to do; confidence allows you to do it.

-Stan Smith

We can never make peace with the outer world until we make peace with ourselves.

-Dalai Lama

He who fears to suffer, suffers from fear.

-French Proverb

Success always demands a greater effort.

-Winston Churchill

Who has confidence himself, will gain the confidence of others.

-Leib Lazarow

There is only one way to happiness and that is to cease worrying about things which are beyond the power of our will.

-Epictetus

A limit on what you will do puts a limit on what you can do.

-Dexter Yager

Happiness can be found in the darkest of times, if one only remembers
to turn on the light.

-J.K. Rowling

It is not only what we do, but also what we do not do,
for which we are accountable.

-Moliere
We grow because we struggle, we learn and overcome.

-R.C. Allen

I find hope in the darkest of days and focus in the brightest.
I do not
judge the universe.

-Dalai Lama

**WHY DO SOME OF US MAKE BAD CHOICES?**
**What were we thinking?**

Research shows that we make over 2,000 decisions per waking hour. They mostly are automatic or instinctive such as what to wear, what to eat for breakfast and day to day choices. Learning how to make good decisions is a good habit to develop. Peering into future outcomes and scenarios will help you make wiser decisions in the present.

Poor choices come from a range of interference at the time of making any decision. One may be overwhelmed or distressed, emotionally out-of-control, panicked, or have a distorted perspective of the situation. It is best not to make any decisions unless you are in a calm state of mind. Wait for the mind to clear and emotions to settle.

Decisions that we should make and don't because of fear of change, money, comfort level, can lead to a worsening situation and much regret.

**Realizing what we *MUST* do to create a better life, to move forward and take the first step is the beginning of a new beginning and a new ending.**

What you may need to make life changing decisions are:

- Courage
- Strength
- Belief in yourself
- Perseverance
- Spiritual Connection
- Balance of the mind
- Understand range of possibilities
- See future outcomes and benefits

- Confidence to make a change and make good things happen to you
- Meditate and think clearly with NO distractions when making choices.
- Emotional Self-control-wait till calm to react and decide
- Prioritize needs and choices to make

Our decisions and choices shape and change our lives.

Questions to ask yourself:

- What do I really need to do?
- What are the steps I should take?
- How much time do I need to organize change? Set goals, dates.
- Why MUST I do this?
- What is the outcome I am looking for? Why?
- What do I need for happiness and purposeful living?
- How do I get peace and comfort?
- Who can help me?
- Who is hindering me?
- What can I do today to help create a better future?
- Are the sacrifices worth it?

**BLOCKERS** TO MAKING GOOD CHOICES need to be changed and or eliminated. You may have one or more of the following blockers that are keeping you from making good life choices to reaching a better path and way of life. First acknowledge which of the blockers you feel are present and then work on releasing and changing them.

- **Laziness** to do what needs to be done.
  Complacency to situation and settling for lower standards.

- **Indecisiveness**-to much advise or information can lead to no choices and confusion. Search within.
- **Dependence on others** -wanting or waiting for someone else's input to create your change.
- **Past Outcomes** – relying on what has happened in past will again happen in future. Stuck in past outcomes.
- **Unprepared** – for unexpected change, job loss, death, accidents, etc.
- **No Strategy**- no plan, no thought for future, no goals - living day-to-day
- **Lack of Self-Confidence**
- **Fear of Unknown**
- **Loss of Faith**
- **Lack of Direction**

WHAT to do?  Search within yourself for what YOU need!
It's your life and you must take control of it.

**Your life is worth thinking about.**

Your life and the way you want to live it comes from decisions made every moment. One can always rearrange and change how things are. Even if a slight change, it's a start. Blaming others for how your life is going can further block you from changing your life.

Blaming your situation is another blocker.  Excuses like: I have kids, I have to work, I can't do anything about it now. EXCUSES are everywhere.  You made those choices to have a family, get married, work at your job, drive the car you have, live where you live etc. Who made you make those choices?

Making the right decisions when going through a difficult traumatic time can be more demanding than you think. It is about knowing you must make choices, be calm minded, takes the steps that will help you move forward and find a better way of living.

I remember sitting and asking myself many of these questions during my own health issue. I knew what I needed to do. I must say I didn't really like what I had to do but it was a MUST. I had to move again, downsize my bills, get my business established, and plan differently for the future. I needed to have a few plans for unexpected illness, unexpected circumstances. I decided to speak to my family about this and a few times each year we go over ideas and future arrangements. We are strategizing, thinking of new ways, without feeling overwhelmed or rushed to make decisions. I found when you at least begin making the effort to organize and better your life, GOD-higher power sends you what you need. Opportunities arise, people are sent to assist you, a feeling of peace and control is within and a feeling of being guided even pushed to a new path is present.

We are all a product of our own decisions. We all have made good and bad choices-but we are to learn from those choices. Take time in the decision- making process, especially during difficult times. Be aware of your choices and how they will affect your present life and your future life.

**EVERYTHING YOU DO TODAY HELPS CREATE TOMMOROW!**

CREATE Your OWN GOAL CHART

Set Goal #1:
WHY is important to reach that goal?
Actions needed to achieve it:
Realistic Timeframe:
Who can help you achieve goal?

Set Goal #2:
WHY is important to reach that goal?
Actions needed to achieve it:
Realistic Timeframe:
Who can help you achieve goal?

Set Goal #3:
WHY is important to reach that goal?
Actions needed to achieve it:
Realistic Timeframe:
Who can help you achieve goal?

Are the goals intertwined? Can you motivate yourself to achieve them or do you need assistance?

As a (Hypnotic) Life Coach I found clients that chose to commit to coaching were highly motivated but also realized they needed help with organizing time, money, and a course of action. Having a well thought out plan and working with a coach will increase your motivation, structure time, and help you stay on course for completing short and long-term goals.

Changing your life and starting new paths will require making choices, changes, strength and the desire to wanting a life back. Wanting to journey the remainder of life - happy, healthy and purposeful. Remember we do have a choice!

# CHAPTER 6

## BECOMING A "NEW" YOU

So, the hard work is done. You've made it! You may not even recognize yourself by now. You have been spiritually awakened, shifted into a new life, have a wider perspective and see all differently, and are changing into a newer version of you. Are you there? Or still transforming?

**How do you become a "new" you and like who you will become?**

You must rid yourself of the old you and move away from where you once were. Let go of the past and move forward. A lot of soul searching is required. *This is your opportunity to emerge any way you choose.* This is what you want for yourself and not what you think others want from you. There is no shortcut to becoming a new version of yourself. It will require a lot of small steps, time, energy, focus, faith and hard work.

Are you:

- Negotiating with yourself and settling?
- Actively learning and making a new pathway for a better life, a better you?
- Working on reaching your full potential?
- Designing your own destiny?
- Clear on what you want and how you want your life to really be?
- Raising your standards and demanding more from yourself?
- Setting goals, planning ahead, working hard?

- Spiritually elevating your soul and listening to what it needs?

What values do you use to define the person you are now?

Who do you really want to be in the future?

What is the goal?

Make life simpler, easier, free from worry. Educate yourself. Learn something new each day. Start with a vision of your future life. Then create a plan on how to attain it. What steps will you need to do? How much time and effort will it require? Take your time and enjoy the process.

I have created a life for myself that I love! I do not need a vacation from my life or work. I had to think of what I need for my happiness, well-being, balance and positive living. It was not one job, but a few. I needed my art career and teaching, my holistic & spiritual practice, piano, and writing. So, I do all. One job was not going to balance my needs for happiness. My home is my sanctuary. My clients feel the peace instantly when they enter. I made it that way. Make your home peaceful, control your space and in time you feel the change occur.

Becoming a new person-a better person is worth the shift. Those who stay the same, settle, or are too lazy or fearful to grow and move forward may find themselves full of regret and unhappy with how life turned out. Not wanting to remain the same and wanting to become more is the mindset one needs for growth and change. If where you are is not how you want it to be, only you can begin the steps to change it. Many small steps will get you there! You can rest along the way but get up and move again. I can honestly say I am exhausted these days and still stick to the routine of writing. It may be less time, but it is still given time.

As you become stronger, confident and empowered you will see the change in yourself and so will others. My sister once said to me that I was not the same person. I said, "I'm not, I am a better version now". I rid myself of an old life and created a new life. It took years and I'm still creating new paths. I have reached a peaceful place. Happy at home, at work, and feeling balanced. A few things linger and I am working on them. Some things can take longer, so be patient.

Part of growth and change is also having faith and spirituality. I live a spiritual path and believe greatly in the power of the Universe, GOD, Angels and Spirit Guides. They speak to us through our souls, send us signs, opportunities, as if out of nowhere. I have had many spiritual experiences that are truly divine intervention. The spiritual path has created the "new" me. I live by this and life seems easier, more rewarding and truly enlightening.

WHAT ARE SPIRITUAL EXPERIENCES?

Have you ever said a prayer and found that it was answered instantaneously? Have you ever had a dream that was a premonition of an event to come? There are some things that happen to us in our lives that modern science fails to explain. These are examples of spiritual experiences that often accompany spiritual practice. Spiritual experiences are given either by the Divine or by negative energies. Spiritual experiences can have a profound effect on your life. You instantly view life differently, finding yourself in awe of divine intervention and wanting to maintain a strong spiritual connection.

I am now a new person from all my spiritual experiences. How can one not be? I feel energy everywhere. From all life. I am in heightened awareness mode all the time. This takes getting used to. The signs sent are clearer and amazing. I feel guided all the time and I follow. My thoughts now manifest easily. It has led me to new paths of education, holistic work, writing books, teaching art and more.

Spiritual connection is an important part of growth. The power of prayer and divine intervention will forever change you and your life. These spiritual interventions and awakenings start this "new" outlook on life. A lot can change after a divine intervention and awakening.
You may:

- Feel different about your job, friends, family, money
- Want to create a new life and an easier more comfortable life
- Need to change careers, go back to school, start a new venture
- Become more spiritual, wanting to learn more, be more fulfilled and live a purposeful life
- Search for purpose and a new direction

It is not easy to become a "New" you. It will require some serious work and effort on your part. It can take some time also. There are some important questions you should ask yourself for each part of your change.

- What is the end goal you are wanting to reach?

- Where do you want to be or doing in 1 year, 2 years? Or more?
- Why do you need to make this change? Knowing WHY is very important! If you can answer the WHY's you will be able to work hard for your goals.
- Why do you want what you want?
- Why will you work for it?
- Why is it priority?
- Why it really needs to be done?
- Why will it make you happier?

Once committed to changing and wanting to create a new life-a new you-the work begins. You will feel wonderful knowing the direction now, for it is what you really want and need to do.

The process of becoming a "new" you can be strange. You may once have liked being out all the time with friends to finding yourself wanting to be around them less. Not that anything is wrong with them you are now just aware that "time" has great value and you will use is more wisely. You may feel pulled to learn more, do more and need to re-arrange time to do these things. Your family and friends may not really like at first who you are changing into. They will need to adjust just the same.

Starting over and rebuilding your life to make life easier, happier, and more fulfilling is worth the journey. It may not go so easy or quick enough but maintain the course and you will surely get there. Attaining a peaceful, happier and purposeful existence is the key to balance. Money should not override this. Of course, figuring out your finances is part of the rebuild, but money should not block you from getting there. Find a way.

Keep what is essential and eliminate everything else.
Declutter your mind, your space, any negativity and start
from scratch if you must.

Starting with a clean slate you may need to move to a new
location, new home, new job, to create this new path and
new ending. I did this and once I decided I was going to I
felt excited to begin the process. I was not in a hurry, just
moving ahead one step at a time. I made new friends,
found new work, enjoyed even the moving process.
Something in my inner soul felt that all this was good and
was exactly what I was supposed to be doing.

All these changes were to get me to the life I wanted. The
state of mind I wanted to be in. The way of life I wanted to
be living.

Becoming a new version of yourself means that you are
using the learnings of your past and planning how you want
your future. This is to make better decisions and
reorganize the plan according to how you want to live your
life.

The process for this in starting my new life was to:
1. First decide on where I wanted to move to and
   what State I wanted live in.
   I **chose** New Jersey. I **chose** near the shore.
2. Deciding on Work-should I maintain some of
   my art jobs while finding new type of
   work…the answer was yes. Then I decided I
   did not want to travel back and forth to New
   York, so I chose to gradually let that work go.
3. I decided to become a Holistic Practitioner.
   Went back to school becoming a Master
   Hypnotherapist, Reiki Master, Life & Spiritual

Coach.  I also still needed my art & piano career and found teaching jobs.

This was the life I wanted.  Blending all that I love to do and working happy.  Creating a life that was fulfilling, enjoyable, stress-free and rewarding.  This was now a balanced life for me.  I am often asked how I do everything.  It is absolutely time management.  Using your time wisely, efficiently, completing tasks and prioritizing.

Some people love sports and watch hours of television where I do not.  My TV time is to relax my mind with a movie or show.  This time is when I need it.  Not planned or routine.  I'll just know I'll need to relax.  *There is nothing on TV that I would miss or rush to watching that is more important than what I do for my own life.*  It is my outlet to rest my body and mind.  If TV time is taking your time, log how many hours in a week you have spent watching TV.  Decide if you need to manage your time differently so that you can work on other goals or take up a hobby you always wanted to do.

TIME is most valuable.  Manage it well and you can attain much more than ever thought you could.

A new "you" should be a better version of you.  You can choose your path, attain balance and a peaceful way of living.  You can now see life clearer and value it differently from your going through difficult times. You may have been through some difficult times and made it through.  You do not worry or stress over the little things anymore.  Living a life simpler and uncomplicated life can created a calmer you. I have created my peaceful and uncomplicated my life and I am grateful for this.  The spiritual shift, the hard work and the desire to achieve this was worth it.

I live a spiritual path. Prayer and allowing divine guidance and intervention to guide me has been highly beneficial to my growth and overall transformation into a better version of myself. Through my difficult period I not only had spiritual growth, but educational and personal growth. While I was recovering from my surgery, I enrolled in an online dog grooming course to learn how to groom my Maltese dog "Romeo". To get certified I had to learn many other breeds, take exams, and then find a grooming establishment that would sponsor me 150 hours of practical hands-on grooming. I decided to finish this and received certification. I also then wrote two books over the next few years while attending the Hypnotherapist program. I seemed to have a sudden urge for education and wanting to expand into other fields. I felt guided for everything. It was wonderful and exciting and further education followed and ongoing. I also went back to showing my art and teaching fine art classes and recently teaching piano again. I juggle many hats, but it all feels wonderful and I feel balanced. That was the goal.

Becoming a "new" you process requires keeping parts of the old you that you want, eliminating what you don't want anymore and then adding the new parts along the way to create your new life. Take your time and think about this. The journey is worth the outcome!

# CHAPTER 7

## FORGIVENESS TO FREEDOM

How to forgive someone who has altered your life, your body, mind and soul in a negative way? It can be one of the most difficult things to do, but one must try. You will be happier afterwards, feeling free this burden you may be carrying around for many years.

If part of your difficult periods have been caused by someone that you hold accountable for how you are, where you are and what you have become, you may want to begin the healing process by spiritually giving this burden to GOD, to higher power. Let it go and be judged another day.

Forgiving those who have done us wrong and caused a spiral of events, a turn for the worse, may be quite difficult. Once you've decided you do not want to carry the burden of hate, disappointment, being blind-sided, taken advantage of, lied to, etc., you will then be able to forgive and let go.

I did forgive my husband for many things that he had been a part of and how I learned about it on the News. Why did he not just confide in me and tell me there were issues coming and we could prepare together? Was I still angry with him? YES. We were not going to get through the difficult period if I did not forgive him. The spiritual path was to understand that a series of events led up to this and I was to help him during this time. I remember someone saying to me if it were my husband in this mess, I would leave him. It hit me hard what I heard. If the circumstances were reversed, I would want him to help me -so I took the spiritual path. Do unto others as you wish they do unto you...popped in my head. So, I remained and helped him.

What is **forgiveness**? ... **Forgiveness** can even lead to feelings of understanding, empathy and compassion for the one who hurt you. **Forgiveness** doesn't mean forgetting or excusing the harm done to you or making up with the person who caused the harm. You don't even have to speak with them to forgive them. This is a forgiveness within yourself- within your soul. **Forgiveness** can bring a kind of peace that helps you go on with life and not obsess to what has happened, to free yourself of negative thoughts and move forward with your life.

Psychologists generally **define forgiveness** as a conscious, deliberate decision to release feelings of resentment or vengeance toward a person or group who has harmed you, regardless of whether they even deserve your **forgiveness**. ... **Forgiveness** does not mean forgetting, nor does it mean condoning or excusing offenses.

The **Bible** has plenty to say about **forgiveness**. ... The Greek word translated as "**forgive**" in the New Testament, aphiēmi, has a wide range of **meanings**, including to remit (a debt), to leave (something or someone) alone, to allow (an action), to leave, to send away, to desert or abandon, ignore, and even to divorce.

TAKE YOUR FREEDOM back! Do not allow yourself to carry any of these negative burdens any longer. Releasing the past and any negativity attached to the past will free you to walk in a new light, on a new path and feel as if reborn again. Close the chapters in your book of life that you no longer want to re-read. No reason to re-read something that will not benefit your future.

Forgiveness is a way to release oneself from a negative thought, judgement or connection.

Forgiveness is a decision to no longer carry or bear this burden.

Forgiveness is about wanting to be free to move forward with a healthier body, mind and soul.

> **If you are struggling to forgive and still cannot find a way, you may need professional care.**
>
> **Please seek *professional counseling* to assist you in the process.**

Part of GETTING YOUR LIFE BACK is releasing yourself from the past, a previous way of living and looking forward on how you need and would like life to start again. We cannot change the past, it is done, completed and we are to either learn from it, let it go, release it, forgive those who may have altered it negatively, and start from TODAY. Start today as if you just were born but with the added knowledge to make wiser decisions for your present life and future life the way you would like it to be.

Many of my family and friends have witnessed my transformation and growth. Seeing an overall transition into my new life, becoming an Author, a Holistic Practitioner, and re-inventing myself and my life. They are amazed to what I have done and often ask for advice on how they can too. I have been spiritually guided and believe it is important to listen to this guidance for making change for the better. Prayer, asking and receiving and then following your intuition will truly transform your life.

My own will and goal to make life better, easier, comfortable and stress-free was the most important thing to me. I watch others now stress and worry to only offer words saying, "there is a better way."

## SPIRITUALITY, FAITH and TRUST

*The better way for me was to take the spiritual path first.* To have faith and trust in GOD and to walk with GOD each day. My belief is unwavering and even through the worst of times I would pray and ask for some relief. One day I remember speaking with GOD and saying, "Really, how long is this going to last? It's been too many years now. I really need this to just end. I need peace again."

That very week everything changed for the better. It felt miraculous.


## BIBLE VERSES TO HELP YOU THROUGH HARD TIMES

### Psalm 37:5

"Commit your way to the Lord. Trust in Him, and He will act."

### Romans 8:18

"For I consider that the sufferings of the present life are not worthy to be compared with the glory that is about to be revealed to us *and* in us!

### Deuteronomy 31:6

"Be strong and courageous, do not be afraid or tremble in dread before them, for it is the Lord your God who goes with you. He will not fail you or abandon you."

### Isaiah 41:10

"Do not fear, for I am with you; Do not be afraid, for I am your God. I will strengthen you, be assured I will help you; I will certainly take hold of you with My righteous hand."

### Joshua 1:9

"Have I not commanded you? Be strong and courageous! Do not be terrified or dismayed, for the Lord your God is with you wherever you go."

### Matthew 6:25-26, 34

25 "Therefor I tell you, stop being worried or anxious about your life, as to what you will eat or what you will drink; nor about your body, as to what you will wear. Is life not more than food, and the body more than clothing?

26 "Look at the birds of the air; they neither sow nor reap nor gather into barns, yet your heavenly Father keeps feeding them. Are you not worth much more than they are?"

34 "So do not worry about tomorrow; for tomorrow will worry about itself. Each day has enough trouble of its own."

# CHAPTER 8

## UNDERSTANDING ONESELF

WHY is it important to understand oneself? Through knowing yourself, you will choose paths that are aligned with your soul and your life purpose. Being altruistic to yourself will overall affect your happiness and well-being. Create a life you are happy and content with, filled with the choices you made to create it.

*Self-awareness* and *deep soul searching* helps us to learn:

- Ones strengths and weaknesses
- What motivates us
- What we need to prioritize
- What is most important to attain positive change in all areas of life
- Who we really are as a person
- Our Life's purpose
- What our dreams are
- What we want to achieve
- About our beliefs and choices

My own life is an example of what is possible and how you can bounce back, regroup, reorganize and reinvent yourself and create the future you want. *I finally found my way back.* It took time. It took years. It was worth it. The spiritual path and strong faith and belief in God and myself has changed my life.

Most people are seeking peace, happiness, success and a stress-free life. But how?

If you want to create your life, you must practice reframing your thoughts into only positive thoughts with positive outcomes. One MUST think about what you are thinking throughout the day. Ask yourself -What do I need and/or want to think about? Make a conscious effort to decide what you want your mind to think about.

What you think about will create your actions and then your actions can create results. The power is within our own minds.

You can reprogram your mind to think positive thoughts. The thoughts you want to have. In hypnosis we learn to reframe our thoughts. As a Master Hypnotherapist this has helped me tremendously. There is always a choice of how we THINK about situations, people and life.

Reframing your thoughts is powerful in its ability to enrich and add to the enjoyment of life instead of walking around always thinking the worst. Reframing negative thoughts to positive thoughts can make people more successful, influential and altogether happier.

**Helpful tools to understanding yourself and where need growth.**

Chart 1

# Wheel of Life
### Finding Balance in Your Life

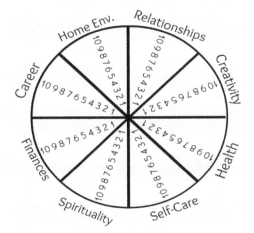

Circle the number that best suits where you are now and to learn what you need to work on for attaining balance in all areas of your life.

10=Fully Satisfied

1 = NOT Satisfied

## Self-Exploration #1 - Q & A

1. LIST ways you dismiss things in your life, things you choose to ignore, bypass, over-criticize.

2. Do you dismiss advice from outside sources? List the some of the reasons WHY you dismiss this advice.

3. What do you believe is keeping you from getting what YOU want?

4. Have you ever failed at something and didn't try again? Would you want to try again?

5. If you reach your goals and dreams and are successful, what would you be afraid of happening?

6. If you have no limitations, would you still want to achieve it?

7. What are you most common EXCUSES you use to avoid taking action in your life?

8. What excuses can you immediately fix? In what ways can you fix them?

- Recognize and banish your excuses.
- Review your Goal Setting plan.
- Monitor your direction, measure the progress.
- Filter fears-address the issues as they arise.
- Use Hypnosis for clearing issues/Self-Clearing techniques.
- Practice Forgiveness-of Yourself and Others and *reframing thoughts*.
- Pose belief that nothing is impossible.

You now know that you *do want* to experience, abundance, love, success, happiness and purposeful living. You are on your way. Changing thoughts and beliefs and maintaining that positive thought process is key. Using methods to amplify what you're able to attract into your life.

YOUR CONSCIOUS MIND has the ability to CHOOSE, ACCEPT and to REJECT. So, WHY would a person accept things they don't want? Or reject things they do want? Because their subconscious mind interferes.

**EMPOWERMENT & POTENTIAL is yours...**

Family, friends, partners, and other outside people can affect your beliefs about your potential and your ability to change for the rest of your life- if YOU ALLOW IT.

You may hear them say or do things such as;

- Quit dreaming
- Get real
- Laugh
- You'll never be able to do that
- Why would you want that?
- Roll their eyes

These things may have already shaped your beliefs. They may continue to be heard while trying to transform your life. YOU CAN CHOOSE to not allow this to affect you or limit you. You can CHOOSE to not be around them. You are in complete CONTROL of your potential, your own destiny, no matter what people say or do. This is the path to true happiness and success.

REFRAMING helps you see things differently. Reframing thoughts, accepting all negative experiences as positive learning experiences, shaping who we are and have become today, realizing the value in all your experiences; both positive and negative.

Bring positive energy into your life immediately, be grateful for what you have in the present moment. Reframe how you see your life as is. Instead of saying, "I'll be grateful when…" -reframe the thought, "I am grateful for..." This is so important to incorporate into your everyday life, allowing to see things in a positive light, bringing positive emotional energy to yourself.

## POWER OF THE MIND

Incorporate as many of the following practices as possible;

- Shift your focus and attention to appreciate the small things of life. Appreciating every small step to your goals.
- Be thankful for all the positive things you have and will have.
- Make time for meditation, spiritual reflections, and/or prayer.
- Take time to be by yourself.
- Practice an 'I can begin again" approach.
- When you feel you simply "can't do it," Seek that person who can, who will show you, help you.
- Reframe negative situations, SEE THE POSITIVE.

## EXERCISE:
## Imagine the Outcome

Focusing on your future, what it could be, what you can accomplish, or be doing helps it to manifest. When you think about them daily, you direct yourself to do the things that will make the events happen.
So, take a few moments each day and imagine the future image of what you desire. SEE it, FEEL it, IMAGINE it!

94

Go through a meditation where you visualize yourself with a NEW way of life, new identity, a new belief system that supports your goals and dreams.

# STRESS EVALUATION CHART

Rate each question as follow;

- 0=Never
- 1=Almost Never
- 2=Sometimes
- 3=Often
- 4=Very Often

How often have you....

1. Felt overwhelmed?
2. Felt anxious?
3. Felt fearful?
4. Felt angry?
5. Felt irritated?
6. Felt frustrated?
7. Felt out of control?
8. Felt somewhat hopeless?
9. Felt depressed?
10. Felt "stuck"?

TOTAL your numbers:

0-10   Below Average: You are handling stress well at the moment.

11-14   Average: Not stress-free, could use some adjustments.

15-18   Medium-High: Whether you are conscious of your stress or not, it's probably affecting your moods, productivity, and relationships.

19+     HIGH: Experiencing high levels of stress, need to address.

IMPORTANT:
*This evaluation is a guide, and NOT meant to replace a medical or psychiatric evaluation.* It is meant to provide insight to where you currently are with your stress load, so that you can take steps to increase balance and wellness in your life.

### Self-Exploration #2 QUESTIONS TO ASK:

1. Are you willing to try new supportive routines? If not, why?
2. Where is your resistance to owning who you are and where you are in life?
3. Are you willing to ask friends to offer their perspectives, for the purpose of exploration and self-discovery?
4. Can you be open to opinions and not take personally?
5. Are you self-aware of your thinking patterns?
6. Are you optimistic or pessimistic?
7. Do you love yourself? If not, why?
8. What do you feel you deserve in life?
9. Are you ready for change?
10. Are you clear on what you want?
11. Are you ready to move up a level? Out of your comfort zone?
12. Are you ready to think positive, attract what you want?
13. DO you want to attract more money?
14. Do you want to succeed?
15. Do you want to fulfill your goals and dreams?
16. Are you willing to work for it? Let nothing get in your way?

### NOURISH YOUR SOUL

Passions fuel your life and nourish your soul. Be empowered to direct your life to be truly fulfilling. Organize your life around your passion, seek joy & fulfillment. You must give meaning to your life and your work…meaning that will inspire, motivate and empower you.

Discover your "why"! This will make your goal, your path clearer, helping you to feel balanced and in harmony. Knowing WHY is key to intentionally creating the life you desire. Another key reason to knowing your WHY is that it is driven by emotions and emotions drive behavior. This WHY empowers you towards effectiveness, efficiency, fulfillment and security. ALWAYS KNOW WHY…

NOW ADD the question WHY? After all of the above question.

## LIFE PURPOSE

It is extremely important to discover, know and understand YOUR life purpose and calling. Living a clear and defined purpose, ensuring happiness and avoiding regrets. Anything that absorbs you, challenges you, gives you a sense of meaning, joy, or passion are the ingredients of purpose and fulfillment.

Purpose is so individual that only you can figure it out, though others can help provide input and guidance. You should just allow yourself to be open to new ideas or inspiration to call upon you. Do not be distracted by society, whatever you pursue for your life purpose is for you to decide.

## SIGNS YOU MAY NOT BE LIVING YOUR HIGHEST PURPOSE IN LIFE

- Not excited to wake up and start your day/work.
- Have mood swings, highs to lows.
- Life is not fulfilling you at all.
- Surrounded by People who bring you down, hold you back.
- Dreams are held back by fears.
- Your present job depletes your energy.

- You feel "stuck" where you are.
- Do not know how to move forward.
- You are not spiritually connected with the universe, God, higher divine power. Loss of faith.

## EXERCISE: FEAR and REGRET

If your life were to end tomorrow, what five things would you regret not doing?...

What

1. _____Wh
   y?_____
2. _____Wh
   y?_____
3. _____Wh
   y?_____
4. _____Wh
   y?_____
5. _____Wh
   y?_____

If your life were to end tomorrow, what five things would make you feel the most guilt?...

1. _____Wh
   y?_____
2. _____Wh
   y?_____
3. _____Wh
   y?_____
4. _____Wh
   y?_____
5. _____Wh
   y?_____

What are you most proud of?

   1.   _____

   2.   _____

   3.   _____

What have you started but never finished?

   1.   _____

   2.   _____

   3.   _____

---

What would you want to complete before you die and why?

---

## LISTEN TO YOUR INNER GUIDANCE

Allow yourself time to relax, meditate, pray, and listen to your inner thoughts. They always have something wise to tell you. Afterwards, write down the thoughts that came to mind. What message can be found? Where are you being directed? What is being asked to do? Spend a week journaling, evaluate and discover more about yourself.

PRACTICE really listening and focusing on the daily events and conversations that happen in your day. What has helped you, what has hindered you? Who has helped you, who has hindered you?

Follow your inner guidance, as it directs you, see what happens. What has changed? Do you feel different? Better? When you go against your inner wisdom, you usually will feel unhappy, questioning a choice you made, wondering why you didn't go with you (gut instinct). The outcome was not what you wanted, and you wished you went with you own inner guidance thoughts and wisdom. WHY, do we repeat this over and over again? BREAK THE HABIT! Begin by LISTENING to your INNER GUIDANCE...follow it and evaluate the outcomes.

SO, as you clear and align yourself with your goals and desires, allow thoughts to direct your path. Pray, meditate, and listen to the divine power, your inner wisdom and act upon inspiration. Take one step at a time, don't count the steps, just concentrate on the step you're working on. Have a clear mind, a clear heart, and a clearing in the fog will appear. Your place of power resides on each individual step you focus on.

Flow with your work, flow with your inspirations, flow with others, flow with divine power, and allow yourself to receive what you deserve.


The process of **self-discovery** is about knowing yourself and the kind of life that you want to experience. Becoming self-aware means becoming more sure of yourself by setting standards and understanding exactly what you want.

**Self-discovery** helps us to identify our abilities, passions and purpose.
**Self-exploration** and **self-discovery** can lead to personal development, personal growth, self-awareness, improvement and understanding.

Understand who you are and the life you want to live.

From this understanding, life changes. Life becomes easier, happier, purposeful and peaceful.

Strong faith and prayer, understanding oneself, deciding how you want to spend the rest of your journey here on earth is the beginning of finding your way.

CPSIA information can be obtained
at www.ICGtesting.com
Printed in the USA
FSHW012031010220
66721FS

9 780578 621395